Nina J. Weinstein

Communication Skits

Illustrated by
Don Robb

Prentice-Hall, Inc., Englewood Cliffs, New Jersey 07632

Library of Congress Cataloging in Publication Data

WEINSTEIN, NINA J.
  Communication skits.

  1. English language—Text-books for foreigners.
2. English language—Conversation and phrase books.
I. Title.
PE1128.W425 1983   428.3′4   82-11265
ISBN   0-13-153569-2

Design, interior layout,
  and production supervision
  by Chrys Chrzanowski
Cover illustration
  by Don Robb
Cover design
  by Judith A. Matz
Manufacturing Buyer:
  Harry P. Baisley

Printed in the United States of America

10   9   8   7   6   5   4   3   2

ISBN   0-13-153569-2

PRENTICE-HALL INTERNATIONAL, INC., *London*
PRENTICE-HALL OF AUSTRALIA PTY. LIMITED, *Sydney*
PRENTICE-HALL CANADA INC., *Toronto*
PRENTICE-HALL OF INDIA PRIVATE LIMITED, *New Delhi*
PRENTICE-HALL OF JAPAN, INC., *Tokyo*
PRENTICE-HALL OF SOUTHEAST ASIA PTE. LTD., *Singapore*
WHITEHALL BOOKS LIMITED, *Wellington, New Zealand*

Contents

**Dedicated to my husband, David,
for not complaining too much**

My sincere thanks to everyone who demonstrated such abundant faith in me during this project. In particular, Sigrid Vivian, Bernice Weiss, Kent Sutherland, Russell Campbell, Diane Larsen-Freeman, and Bertie Wood encouraged and supported the project above and beyond the call of duty.

For her careful, meticulous handling of the myriad of details that comprised the production of this book, I would like to sincerely thank Chrys Chrzanowski, my production editor. And for her support, backing, and enthusiasm, I'd like to thank our beautiful ESL editor, Marianne Russell.

Most especially, I would like to thank Tina Carver, without whom I might never have finished *Communication Skits*.

Preface

Communication Skits offers a multitude of conversational games and exercises to teach and stimulate ESL students. It encourages the practice of real communication: exchanging ideas, debating, arguing, teaching, learning, and enjoying the give and take inherent in conversation. The skits can be taught as conversations or enacted following stage directions and using suggested props. Enactment allows students to physically demonstrate their understanding of the material while changing the classroom focus from studying about English to using English as a living, breathing tool of communication.

Organization

There are six units. Each unit contains three skits based on a similar topic and is accompanied by cartoon-like art to give students a visual representation of the content of the skit. The first two skits set the theme with structured dialogues, new vocabulary (in the context of the skit), and discussion questions. Students practice the skits and exercises from the first two skits and then create a third skit based upon the vocabulary and ideas they have been learning and generating. The sixth unit allows students to demonstrate what they have learned from the entire book.

Exercises

New vocabulary is approached inductively. Graded exercises emphasize partner work. The vocabulary is important, but it is not an end in and of itself; rather, the intent is to focus on obtaining information from a partner by using the vocabulary as a new-found tool.
The vocabulary exercises utilize a three dot grading system: One dot (●) indicates the easiest exercises, two dots (●●) indicate those that are more challenging, and three dots (●●●) are the most difficult, or communicative, exercises.

Comprehension questions test the students' ability to understand the context of the skit. The last question of each Comprehension Section allows students to show their understanding of the skit by restating it in their own words. They are always given a few sentences to help them get started.

Communicating Your Feelings gives students the opportunity to discover and practice correct forms of expression in formal and informal situations. Often degrees of intensity are explained, such as: "I'm hot/I'm boiling/I'm about to burn up."

One Step Further is a culmination of the previous exercises in the chapter. It is meant to be thought-provoking and fun. Students work in groups and explore an idea, fact, or opinion brought up in the skit. For instance, the skit "Taxes, Taxes, Taxes" suggests that taxes are high for the average American. In *One Step Further*, one question deals with the practical side of taxes from the perspective of the budget makers. Students are assigned the task of creating a budget for a new country. They are given suggested expenditures and thus encouraged to think through and discuss the realities of taxation.

The ESL Game serves as a review of vocabulary from the skits. Its intent is to involve all the students in group-oriented active participation, to encourage learning through team effort, and to give practice in thinking quickly and effectively in English. The clue cards and posters can be torn from the book, and the clue cards should be cut apart. One set can be used for the entire class.

But How Do You Teach a Skit?

Teaching a skit is easy and fun. Each group learns differently, but the following can serve as a basis for ideas on how students can most effectively learn communication through skits:

1. Read the skit to the class using suggested props and *demonstrating* stage directions. (Don't read them.) Students can repeat the skit line-by-line during a second reading.
2. Reinforce the vocabulary. This can be done either before or after the reading.
3. Now break the class into groups according to the number of parts to be played. If there are five characters, each group should have five people. Have the students practice reading their lines *meaningfully*. The stage directions in parentheses should be done, not read. Upon finishing the first reading, students should change roles and read the skit again. This procedure should continue until each group member has read each part.
4. Walk around the room during this time helping each group.
5. When each group has practiced sufficiently, the class can reconvene. Volunteers from each group or an entire volunteer group can enact the skit using the appropriate props. This enactment can be done from the students' seats or in front of the class, depending on the preference of the particular group.

The book's organization is purposely simple. Its intent is to have students internalize the English language, produce meaningful and spontaneous conversations, and last, but not least, to have a good time with their new language.

Nina J. Weinstein

1

Communication Tools

YOU REALLY HAVE A WAY WITH WORDS

Props: a newspaper.

Scene: Gina and Dan are having breakfast. Dan is reading the newspaper.

Gina: I'm really worried about <u>inflation</u>. I was listening to the radio yesterday and they said inflation increased by 10 percent last year. What do you think?

Dan: (*Without looking up*) <u>Huh</u>?

Gina: I said I'm worried about inflation. I'm going shopping this afternoon and I know the price of beef will be higher than last month. (*Seriously*) Do you think the <u>economy</u> is going to improve?

Dan: (*Turning the page*) <u>Uh uh</u>.

Gina: Why not? This is an election year and the economy always improves in an election year.

Dan: <u>Uh huh</u>.

Gina: (*A little excited*) And the <u>prime interest rate</u> is going down.

Dan: <u>Hmmm</u>.

Gina: (*More excited*) And businesses will be looking for <u>alternative energy sources</u>. That should cut <u>operating</u> costs.

Dan: <u>Mmmm</u>.

Gina: (*Impatient*) Well, what do you think?

Dan: (*Finishing the newspaper*) <u>Huh</u>?

COMPREHENSION

Answer the following questions with your class.

1. What is Gina worried about?
2. What is Dan's reaction?
3. When does the economy usually improve? Why do you think the economy improves at that time?
4. What rate is going down?
5. Why should businesses look for energy alternatives?
6. What is Dan's final comment? Why do you think he reacts that way?
7. What country do you think Gina and Dan are from? Why?
8. How long do you think Gina and Dan have been married? Why?
9. Restate the skit in your own words. Use the illustration to help you. **(Tell what happened. Example: First, Gina said she was worried about inflation. She asked Dan what he thought. He continued to read the newspaper, etc.)**

USING VOCABULARY TO COMMUNICATE

INFORMAL SPOKEN ENGLISH

Conversational "Noises"	Usual Meanings(s)
Huh?	What? (What did you say?)
Uh uh.	No.
Uh huh.	Yes.
Hmmm.	I'm thinking. Very interesting.
Mmmm.	Yes. I'm thinking. Very interesting. Very tasty (food). I agree.

Repeat the above conversational "noises" after your teacher.

● WORK WITH A PARTNER. Respond to the following statements by using the appropriate conversational "noises".

1. **Partner:** This is delicious.
   You: Mmmm.

2. **You:** There's the President.
   Partner: _____

3. **Partner:** I think gold is the safest investment you can make.

   You: _____

4. **You:** Do you think world peace is possible?

   Partner: _____

5. **Partner:** Are you going to a party tonight?

   You: _____

MORE VOCABULARY

> **inflation**
> **alternative energy sources**
> **prime interest rate**
> **economy**
> **operating (verb: to operate)**

•• NOW CHANGE PARTNERS. Some of the words below are underlined. Substitute the vocabulary words which have the same meaning as the underlined words. Then ask your partner each of the questions. When you finish, have your partner question you.

1. If you could, what would you do to control the increase in the amount of money but the decrease in its value?

   Question: If you could, what would you do to control inflation?

   Answer: I would decrease spending and increase productivity.

2. How would you decrease the running expenses of businesses?

   Question: _____

   Answer: _____

3. What other forms of power are available?

   Question: _____

   Answer: _____

4. How can we improve the management of the country's money?

   Question: _____

   Answer: _____

5. What is the current percentage banks charge their best customers to borrow money?

   Question: _____

   Answer: _____

••• CHANGE PARTNERS AGAIN. Finish the following sentences using your own ideas.

1. Inflation is _____ .

2. A good <u>alternative energy source</u> _____ .

3. The <u>prime interest rate</u> _____ .

4. The <u>economy</u> _____ .

5. <u>Operating expenses must</u> _____ .

COMMUNICATING YOUR FEELINGS—AN EXPANSION EXERCISE

WORK WITH A PARTNER. Follow the instructions preceding each sentence or exchange.

1. Your partner just said something that makes you worried. Say your partner's name so that he or she knows you're worried.

   "_____ ."
   　(name)

2. Your partner is going to ask you a question. If you can answer correctly, you'll win a new car. Say, "I know! I know the answer!" so that he or she knows you're excited.

   Partner: The question is, "How many meters are in a kilometer?"
   You: (*Excited*) I know! I know the answer!

3. Your partner just failed a test. You're his teacher and you have to tell him gently. He answers sadly.

   You: (*Gently*) You didn't do very well on the test. But don't worry. You'll do better next time.
   Partner: (*Sadly*) Oh no.

4. There's a rule that you can't chew gum in class. You think your partner is chewing gum. You question her suspiciously. She answers innocently.

   You: (*Suspiciously*) Are you chewing gum?
   Partner: (*Innocently*) No. I'm biting my lip because I'm nervous.

5. Your partner is sick. He doesn't want anyone to know. He quietly asks you to help him. You answer softly.

   Partner: (*Quietly*) I'm sick. Would you walk to the restroom with me?
   You: (*Softly*) Sure.

ONE STEP FURTHER

Discuss the following questions in small groups. Choose a discussion leader to report back to the class when you finish.

1. Situation: A friend is talking to you, but you're thinking about

something else. All of a sudden, you realize your friend is waiting for your opinion. You don't know what to say.

Have you ever been in the above situation? How can you be a better listener?

2. Your friend is trying to talk to you. You're busy and don't want to talk right now. How can you tell your friend without hurting his feelings?

3. Do you have conversational "noises" in your native language? Give your native language's equivalent for

huh? _____

uh uh _____

uh huh _____

hmmm _____

mmmm _____

What other conversational "noises" are there in your native language?

4. Group activity: Write a conversation using the following conversational "noises": huh, uh uh, uh huh, hmmm, mmmm.

5. Group activity: The following are popular conversational topics. List them in order of their interest to your group (the most interesting first; the least, last).

Politics   1. _____

Love   2. _____

Money   3. _____

School   4. _____

Friendship   5. _____

Sex   6. _____

Jobs (careers)   7. _____

Household topics (children,
    cooking, cleaning, etc.)   8. _____

Dating   9. _____

Music   10. _____

Literature   11. _____

Movies   12. _____

BUT THAT'S NOT WHAT I MEANT

Props: coffee cups, dishes, notepad for waitress, coffee pot.

Scene: Aiko, Shozo, and Mikio are Japanese. They are having their first dinner at an American restaurant with their American friend, Tim. They are sitting by the window.

Tim: (*To Aiko after they've both had three cups of coffee*) I don't want another cup of coffee. Do you?

Aiko: (*She <u>nods</u> "yes," meaning in her culture, "No, I don't."*)

Tim: (*Surprised*) You do? (*He calls the waitress.*) Waitress. Waitress!

Waitress: (*To Aiko*) More coffee? (*She begins to pour.*)

Aiko: No, thank you.

Waitress: Oh. I'm sorry.

Tim: (*To Shozo, who's had two dishes of ice cream*) You don't want another dish of ice cream, do you?

Shozo: (*He nods "yes," meaning in his culture, "No, I don't."*)

Waitress: You do? Okay. One dish of ice cream. (*She leaves.*)

Tim: (*Pointing to the street in front of the restaurant.*) There's John from our math class. Please invite him to join us. I'll be right back.
(*Shozo and Mikio use the Japanese <u>gesture</u>, "Come here," to get their friend's attention. Unfortunately this gesture looks like the American gesture for "hello." John <u>waves</u> "hello" and then leaves.*)

Shozo: Where's he going?

Mikio: I don't know. (*Aiko leaves.*)

Tim: (*Tim returns and says to Mikio*) Do you know where Aiko is? <u>One minute she was here and the next minute she was gone.</u>

Mikio: (*He moves his right hand back and forth in front of his face for the Japanese gesture, "I don't know."*)

Tim: Are there flies in here? (*He looks around.*)

Shozo: There's Aiko. She looks lost. Aiko, come here. (*She doesn't hear.*)

Tim: (He gestures "come here" with his right index finger. Aiko looks puzzled.)
Aiko: Tim, we don't use that gesture in Japan. It's not polite.
Tim: (Apologetically) But that's not what I meant...

Tim: (*He gestures "Come here" with his right index finger. Aiko looks puzzled.*)

Aiko: (*As she's sitting*) Tim, we don't use that gesture in Japan. It's not polite.

Tim: (*Apologetically*) But that's not what I meant . . . .

COMPREHENSION

Answer the following questions with your class:

1. Where are Aiko, Mikio, and Shozo from?
2. Who are they having their first American dinner with?
3. In Aiko's culture you nod in agreement if someone makes a negative statement.

   Example: Tim: I don't want another cup of coffee. Do you?
   Aiko: Yes.

   She's saying, "Yes. You're right. I don't want another cup of coffee." In your native culture, do people nod in agreement to a negative statement? If not, how would they respond to Tim's question if they didn't want more coffee?
4. When Shozo and Mikio gesture for John to "come here," he leaves. Why? What is the gesture for "come here" in your native culture?
5. Shozo uses the Japanese gesture for "I don't know." Why does Tim ask if there are flies in the room? What is the gesture for "I don't know" in your native culture?
6. Why is Aiko upset with Tim?
7. Restate the skit in your own words. Use the illustration to help you. **(Tell what happened. Example: First, Tim asks Aiko if she wants more coffee. She nods. . . .)**

USING VOCABULARY TO COMMUNICATE:

gesture
to nod
to wave
apologetically (to apologize)
One minute she was here and the next minute she was gone.

● WORK WITH A PARTNER. Use all five vocabulary words and expressions from above. Fill in the blanks, one letter for each blank. Make each vocabulary word agree in tense and person with its sentence. You and your partner should agree on each answer.

1. When Tim asks if Aiko wants coffee, she __ __ __ __ . She really doesn't want any.
2. Shozo and Mikio use the wrong __ __ __ __ __ __ __ to get their friend's attention.
3. John __ __ __ __ __ "hello" and then leaves.

4. When Tim comes back, he notices Aiko is gone. He says, "_ _ _ _ _ _ _ _ _

_ _ _ _ _ _ _ _ _ _ _ _ _ _ _ _ _ _ _

_ _ _ _ _ _ _ _ _ _ _ _ _ _ _ _ _ ."

5. When Aiko tells Tim his _ _ _ _ _ _ _ is impolite, Tim answers very

_ _ _ _ _ _ _ _ _ _ _ _ _ _ _ _ .

● ● WORK WITH A PARTNER. Some of the words below are underlined. Substitute the vocabulary words which have the same meaning as the underlined words. Then ask your partner each of the questions. When you finish, have your partner question you.

1. What movement does your partner use to say "good-bye"?

Question: _____

Answer: _____

2. Does she move her head up and down to say "yes"?

Question: _____

Answer: _____

3. Does your partner hold up his hand and move it back and forth to say "hello"?

Question: _____

Answer: _____

4. Does your partner ever have to say she's sorry for using the wrong body language?

Question: _____

Answer: _____

5. Does your partner leave suddenly, causing people to say he was here a minute ago?

Question: _____

Answer: _____

● ● ● NOW CHANGE PARTNERS. Finish the following sentences by using your own ideas.

1. My partner nods his head _____ .

2. My partner's favorite foreign gesture is _____ .

3. The last time I saw someone wave was _____ .

4. _____ . One minute she was

here and the next minute she was gone.

5. My partner apologizes _____ .

COMMUNICATING YOUR FEELINGS—AN EXPANSION EXERCISE

WORK WITH A PARTNER. Follow the instructions preceding each sentence or exchange.

1. You accidentally step on your partner's foot. Say "I'm sorry" apologetically.

    You: (*Apologetically*) I'm sorry.
    Partner: That's okay.

2. Your partner is your teacher. He says you just got the best grade in the class on yesterday's test. Answer, showing your surprise.

    Partner: (*Happy*) You just got the best grade in the class!
    You: (*Surprised*) I did?

3. Your partner explains something to you that is very confusing.

    Partner: If you say, "I don't want dessert, do you?" to a Japanese person and he doesn't want dessert either, he'll say, "Yes." This means he agrees with what you said.
    You: (*Confused*) Huh?

4. Your partner tells you some surprising information.

    Partner: I'm actually related to the Queen of England.
    You: (*Surprised*) Really?

5. You say something that hurts your partner's feelings.

    You: (*Apologetically*) But that's not what I meant. . . .

ONE STEP FURTHER

Discuss the following questions in small groups. Choose a discussion leader to report back to the class when you finish.

Restaurant Etiquette[1]

1. In the United States
    a. a woman walks in front of a man in a restaurant. Compare this to your native culture.
    b. a hostess seats the customers. Compare this to your native culture.
    c. a man (or the waiter) can help a woman into her chair. Compare this to your native culture.
    d. a man can order for a woman. Compare this to your native culture.
    e. a man usually pays for the check. Compare this to your native culture.
    f. a man can help a woman put on her coat. Compare this to your native culture.
    g. a man can open the car door for a woman. Compare this to your native culture.

2. In the United States
    a. the salad is usually served on one dish and the meat, potatoes, and vegetable on another. Compare this to your native culture.

[1] Etiquette: behavior in social situations; social manners.

     b. you can use your fingers to eat fried chicken and ribs. When can you use your fingers to eat in your native culture?

     c. a fork, knife, and spoon are used to eat. What is used in your native culture?

     d. a napkin is usually placed on the lap during the meal. Compare this to your native culture.

3. In the United States

     a. a tip (money) is usually left for the waiter or waitress. Compare this to your native culture.

     b. if the service and food are very good, the tip can be larger. Compare this to your native culture.

     c. if the service and food are bad, the tip can be small, or there may be no tip. Compare this to your native culture.

4. What is the strangest foreign food you've ever eaten? Did you like it?

5. Group activity: First have your teacher demonstrate the American body language gestures for the following:

     a. Me?

     b. You.

     c. Yes.

     d. No.

     e. I don't know. *(+ I don't care)*

     f. Hurry! *Perfect.*

     g. Stop.

     h. Come here.

     i. He's crazy.

     j. Please move.

     k. Hello.

     l. Good-bye. *M. Oh no, I forgot!* *I don't like it (wrinkle nose)*

Now give each body language gesture in your own native culture.

THE DATE

Finish writing this skit in a small group (five or more people). Try to use body language and as many conversational "noises" as you can.

Props: fill in as needed.

Scene: Richard and Tina are in the same class at school. Richard wants to ask Tina for a date. He's having problems knowing what to say.

After School

Richard: (*To Tina*) Wasn't that an interesting class?

Tina: Huh?

Richard: I said, 'Wasn't that an interesting class?'

Tina: (*She nods.*) Uh huh.

Richard: _____

Tina: _____

Richard: _____

Tina: _____

Richard: _____

Tina: _____

Richard: _____

Tina: _____

Richard: _____

Tina: _____

Richard: _____

COMPREHENSION

Answer the following questions with your class.

1. Describe each group's skit in your own words.

2. Which solution to the "problem" do you think is best? Why?

ONE STEP FURTHER

Discuss the following questions in small groups. Choose a discussion leader to report back to the class when you finish.

1. In the United States it's possible for women to ask men for a date. How do you feel about this? Is it possible in your native country?

2. Tell what native country you're from and then role-play (with a volunteer) a man asking a woman for a date.

3. What do single people from your native country look for in each other?

4. Describe a perfect date. Tell where you went, describe your partner, etc.

5. As a class, make a one-page questionnaire for potential "dates" to fill out. Include the things that are important for two people to have in common. Possible questions include the following:

   1. What is your name?
   2. Are you male or female?
   3. What do you do?
   4. How old are you?
   5. What are your hobbies?
   6. How tall are you?

   Do you like to dance?

   Everyone in class should fill out the questionnaire. Now divide into groups of ten or fewer. Have the teacher collect the questionnaires, mix them up, and then give ten or fewer to each group. Each group should find a perfect partner for each applicant based on the information in the questionnaire.

USING VOCABULARY TO COMMUNICATE

Play The ESL Game.

THE ESL GAME—RULES

1. The class is divided into two teams.

2. Six topics are written on the blackboard.

3. Two players from one team come up and face each other.

4. The players decide which topic they want. A topic can be used only once. As topics are chosen, they are erased from the board.

5. The players decide who gives and who receives the clues. The person who gives the clues receives the Small Clue Card for the topic chosen.

6. The clue-giver uses synonyms, antonyms, definitions, descriptions, etc., to get his partner to guess the words.

7. A student is chosen to keep track of the time. Each team is allowed one minute. With a more advanced class, the time can be shortened to thirty seconds.

8. A student is chosen to hold up the Poster for the topic so the class can follow.

9. The class must be quiet. If students yell out answers, their team loses the point.

10. Instruct the clue-giver not to use any language but English or he'll lose the point. He must follow the order given on the Small Clue Card. If he wants to skip a word, he must say, "I'm skipping Number 2." If he doesn't, he loses the point.

11. The timekeeper begins the game by saying "begin" and ends it one minute later by saying "stop."

12. The players get one point for every answer correctly guessed. An answer correctly guessed is the exact word or words on the Small Clue Card.

13. The game is continued with two players from the next team.

14. When all the topics are chosen, the team with the most points wins.

SMALL CLUE CARDS*

*Easy Vocabulary (from
"You Really Have a Way
with Words")*

1. breakfast
2. newspaper
3. month
4. shopping
5. election
6. afternoon

Body Language

1. Yes
2. I don't know
3. No
4. Come here
5. Good-bye
6. Hello

Body Language

1. Me?
2. Hurry
3. You
4. Stop
5. He's crazy
6. Please move

Conversational "Noises"

1. huh
2. uh uh
3. uh huh
4. mmmm
5. hmmm
6. uh uh

The Economy

1. economy
2. alternative energy sources
3. prime interest rate
4. inflation
5. operating
6. operate

Feelings

1. excited
2. worried
3. sad
4. happy
5. surprised
6. apologetic

* *Note:* Tear out this page and cut out the clue cards.

EASY VOCABULARY (from "You Really Have a Way With Words)"

1. BREAKFAST

2. NEWSPAPER

3. MONTH

4. SHOPPING

5. ELECTION

6. AFTERNOON

BODY LANGUAGE

1. YES

2. I DON'T KNOW

3. NO

4. COME HERE

5. GOOD – BYE

6. HELLO

BODY LANGUAGE

1. ME?

2. HURRY

3. YOU

4. STOP

5. HE'S CRAZY

6. PLEASE MOVE

CONVERSATIONAL NOISES

1. HUH

2. UH UH

3. UH HUH

4. M M M M

5. HMMM

6. UH UH

22

THE ECONOMY

1. ECONOMY

2. ALTERNATIVE ENERGY SOURCES

3. PRIME INTEREST RATE

4. INFLATION

5. OPERATING COSTS

6. OPERATE

FEELINGS

1. EXCITED

2. WORRIED

3. SAD

4. HAPPY

5. SURPRISED

6. APOLOGETIC

2

Money or a Lack
Thereof

TAXES, TAXES, TAXES

Props: a check.

Scene: Today is payday for Ken.

Bookkeeper: I just finished <u>figuring out</u> your check. I want to go over it together so there'll be no misunderstandings.[1]

Ken: Okay. (*They look at the check together.*)

Bookkeeper: You <u>grossed</u> $600.00.

Ken: (*Very happy*) Fantastic! I just bought a new refrigerator <u>on credit</u> for my wife's birthday. Now I can pay for it.

Bookkeeper: I took $7.50 out for your <u>union dues</u>.

Ken: Fine.

Bookkeeper: Then I found out you borrowed $5,000 from the <u>credit union</u>. Your payment for that was $100.00.

Ken: Okay.

Bookkeeper: <u>Disability</u> came to $6.00 and your savings plan[2] was $50.00.

Ken: (*A little upset*) Can I have my check now?

Bookkeeper: Just a minute. Then I had <u>to deduct</u> $90.30 for <u>federal</u> taxes, and $13.18 went to the <u>state</u>.

Ken: (*He sits down*) I'd better take the refrigerator back.

Bookkeeper: Whoops! I forgot our new city tax. (*He figures it out.*) That comes to $10.98.

Ken: (*Very weak*) I guess we can move to a smaller apartment. Are you finished yet?

Bookkeeper: Not quite.[3] <u>Social Security</u> cost you another $36.78.

Ken: (*Softly*) Oh no.

Bookkeeper: (*He hands Ken a check for $285.26.*) Here. See you in two weeks.

[1] Misunderstandings: wrong ideas.
[2] Savings plan: a special savings account employees can have through their companies.
[3] Not quite: not yet.

COMPREHENSION

Answer the following questions with your class.

1. What did the bookkeeper just finish doing?
2. Why does he want to go over the check with Ken?
3. How much did Ken gross?
4. What did he just buy on credit? Why?
5. How much was the first deduction? How did Ken react to it?
6. How much was the credit union deduction? The savings plan?
7. What did disability come to? Federal taxes? State taxes?
8. How much was the city tax? Social Security?
9. The bookkeeper finally gave Ken his check. How much was it?
10. Restate the skit in your own words. Use the illustration to help you. (Tell what happened. Example: The bookkeeper wanted to go over Ken's check. Ken grossed $600.00, etc.)

amount to
add up to; =

USING VOCABULARY TO COMMUNICATE

social security   federal
union dues   on credit
credit union   to figure out
state   to gross
disability   to deduct

● WORK WITH A PARTNER. Use all ten vocabulary words from above. Fill in the blanks, one letter for each blank. Make each vocabulary word agree in tense and person with its sentence. You and your partner should agree on each answer.

The bookkeeper was _ _ _ _ _ _ _ _   _ _ _ Ken's check. Ken

_ _ _ _ _ _ _ $600.00.

First the bookkeeper _ _ _ _ _ _ _ _ _ $7.50 for _ _ _ _ _

_ _ _ _ _ . Then Ken had to pay $100.00 to the _ _ _ _ _ _   _ _ _ _ _ .

_ _ _ _ _ _ _ _ _ _ _ came to $6.00, and $13.18 went to the _ _ _ _ _ _ .

_ _ _ _ _ _ _ taxes came to $90.30. _ _ _ _ _ _

_ _ _ _ _ _ _ _ was $36.78.

Ken bought a refrigerator _ _   _ _ _ _ _ _ . He wanted to pay for it. Now

he'd have to wait.

●● WORK WITH A PARTNER. Read the following explanations of United States taxes. Then ask your partner each question. When you finish, have your partner question you.

1. *Disability insurance:* a tax employees pay to the state government. If the employee becomes too sick to work for a long period of time, he can receive a check every two weeks[1] from the state government. If the employee can't work because he had an accident away from work, he can also receive money from disability insurance.

---

[1] This varies from state to state.

Do they have disability insurance in your native country? Explain.

2. *Federal tax:* a tax every employee pays to the United States (federal) government. Federal tax is the largest tax an employee pays.

Do you pay federal tax in your native country? Explain.

3. *State tax:* a tax employees pay to the state government. Some states don't have any state tax.

Is there state tax in your native country? Explain.

4. *Social Security:* a tax employees pay to the United States government for many years. When an employee retires (reaches a certain age and stops working), he receives a monthly check from the federal government until he dies.

Is there Social Security in your native country? Explain.

5. *Union dues:* money a worker pays to belong to and maintain membership in a union. A union is a group of workers in the same profession who work together for better job conditions.

Do you know anyone who belongs to a union? Explain.

6. *Credit union:* a financial corporation for employees of a company who pay a membership fee only or pay a membership fee and belong to a union (depends on the particular rules of the credit union). An employee can usually borrow money at a lower rate of interest from the credit union than from the bank.

Do they have credit unions in your native country? Explain.

•• NOW CHANGE PARTNERS. Some of the words below are underlined. Substitute the vocabulary words which have the same meaning for the underlined words. Then ask your partner each of the questions. When you finish, have your partner question you.

7. How much would they take out from a $600 paycheck in your native country?
   Question: How much would they deduct from a $600 paycheck in your native country?

   Answer: _____

8. How much does an average worker earn before taxes in your native country?

   Question: _____

   Answer: _____

9. Is it difficult to do the arithmetic for a paycheck in your native country?

   Question: _____

   Answer: _____

10. Do many people <u>buy now and pay later</u> in your native country?

    Question: Do many people buy _____ in your native country?
                                       (Vocabulary)

    Answer: _____

●●● Find a classmate who works. What deductions are taken out of the paycheck? Can you explain each deduction?

COMMUNICATING YOUR FEELINGS—AN EXPANSION EXERCISE

DEGREES OF INTENSITY (INFORMAL)

Average	*Intense*	*Very Intense*

That's good.
    fine.
    nice.
    very nice.
	That's great.
	    wonderful.
	    exciting.
		That's fantastic!
		    fabulous!
		    thrilling!
		    stupendous!
		    very exciting!
		    incredible!

Repeat the above "Degrees of Intensity" after your teacher.

WORK WITH A PARTNER. Respond to the following statements using (in your opinion) the appropriate level of intensity.

1. **Partner:** I just bought a new car!
   You: <u>That's great.</u>

2. **Partner:** I'm getting married next month!
   You: _____

3. **Partner:** We're buying a new television!
   You: _____

4. **Partner:** My uncle just won a lot of money!
   You: _____

5. **Partner:** I'm graduating from college next week!
   You: _____

6. **You:** My (wife/husband) and I are going to have a baby!
   Partner: _____

7. **You:** We're going to Hawaii on vacation!
   Partner: _____

8. **You:** I'm going to visit my family next month!
   Partner: _____

9.   **You:** My teacher told me my English is improving!

    Partner: _____

10. **You:** My dentist told me my teeth are all fine!

    Partner: _____

ONE STEP FURTHER

Discuss the following questions in small groups. Choose a discussion leader to report back to the class when you finish.

1. Americans buy on credit. What do you think about this?

2. Governments often spend more money than they have. This is called deficit spending. Can governments continue to do this? Why or why not?

3. Do you think the government wastes money? If so, on what?

4. Are taxes too high? If so, what can we do to lower them?

5. Group activity: Your group has just started a new country. The first thing you must do is make a budget for the country. How will you spend your money? What percentage (%) of your country's money will you spend on each item? Why? (Your entire budget should add up to 100 percent.)

Education	_____%
Defense	_____%
Space travel	_____%
Foreign aid	_____%
Health	_____%
New housing for poor	_____%
Job training for poor	_____%
Redevelopment of large cities	_____%
Welfare	_____%
Transportation	_____%
Social Security	_____%
Other	
_____	_____%
_____	_____%
_____	_____%
_____	_____%

THE PERFECT CAR

Props: None.

Scene: Mrs. Kent is shopping for a used car.

Mrs. Kent: (*To the salesperson*) I'm looking for a used car. I need a reliable car that gets good gas mileage.

Salesperson: (*Excited*) I have the perfect car for you. Please follow me to the back of the lot. (*Mrs. Kent follows him to the back of the car lot.*)

Salesperson: Well. (*Pointing*) Here she[1] is.

Mrs. Kent: She? (*Looks around*) Who?

Salesperson: The car. She's a beauty. And she's only got 40,000 miles.

Mrs. Kent: What year is . . . (*Hesitantly*) she?

Salesperson: She's a 1965.

Mrs. Kent: How does she run?

Salesperson: (*Energetically*) Like a sewing machine.

Mrs. Kent: May I drive her?

Salesperson: Certainly.

Mrs. Kent: (*She tries to start the car three times, but it won't start.*) I'm afraid it won't start.

Salesperson: You've got to give her a little kick right here. (*He kicks the car.*) Now try it.

Mrs. Kent: (*The car starts.*) Hmmm. (*Looking in the rearview mirror*) What's all that smoke back there? (*She points.*)

Salesperson: Oh, all of these older cars smoke. It's nothing. But if I were you, I'd get a complete overhaul as soon as possible.

Mrs. Kent: (*She drives around the car lot.*) (*Stopping in front of the salesperson*) I'm very sorry, but I think something dropped off while I was driving.

Salesperson: (*He checks the car.*) Oh. If I were you, I wouldn't worry. It was only the muffler.

---

[1] She: Using the pronoun "she" shows affection for the car.

Mrs. Kent: It is a little noisy now.

Salesperson: (*Yells*) What?

Mrs. Kent: (*Yells*) It's noisy. I'll turn off the engine.

Salesperson: (*Yells*) What?

Mrs. Kent: (*Yells*) The engine. (*She turns it off.*)

Salesperson: (*He opens the door for Mrs. Kent and she gets out.*) Look at these tires. They're the car's original tires.

Mrs. Kent: They look a little bald.

Salesperson: Well, if I were you, I'd buy new tires. I really would.

Mrs. Kent: How's the gas mileage?

Salesperson: Well, it could be better. I think it's the carburetor. If I were you, I'd get that fixed right away. Gas is expensive.

Mrs. Kent: Well, how much do you want for this car?

Salesperson: Oh, we could give it to you for $4,000.

Mrs. Kent: (*Shocked*) $4,000? I only want to drive it to and from the market. And maybe to my son's house once a week.

Salesperson: (*Excited*) Oh! Why didn't you say so? I've got the perfect motorcycle for you! She's a beauty. Only 100,000 miles, but if I were you. . . .

COMPREHENSION

Answer the following questions with your class.

1. What kind of car does Mrs. Kent need?
2. The salesperson shows her a car. How many miles does it have?
3. What year is it?
4. What does he mean by "[She runs] like a sewing machine"?
5. Why does the car smoke?
6. What dropped off the car while Mrs. Kent was driving? Why is the car noisy now?
7. How are the tires?
8. What's wrong with the carburetor?
9. Why does the salesperson show Mrs. Kent a motorcycle?
10. Restate the skit in your own words. Use the illustration to help you. (**Tell what happened. Example: First, Mrs. Kent told the salesperson what kind of car she wanted. Then . . .**)

USING VOCABULARY TO COMMUNICATE

carburetor	bald
gas mileage	to overhaul (*n*: overhaul)
engine	to run
muffler	to say so *tell somebody*
car lot	to have _____ miles

● WORK WITH A PARTNER. Use all ten vocabulary words and expressions from above. Fill in the blanks, one letter for each blank. Make each vocabulary word and expression agree in tense and person with its sentence. You and your partner should agree on each answer.

1. The salesperson takes Mrs. Kent to the back of the _ _ _ _ _ _ .

2. He shows her a car that _ _ _ _ _ _ _ _ _ _ _ _ _ .

3. He says the car _ _ _ _ like a sewing machine.

4. But it needs an _ _ _ _ _ _ _ _ _ .

5. And the _ _ _ _ _ _ _ fell off.

6. Mrs. Kent turns off the _ _ _ _ _ _ because it's so noisy.

7. The car gets poor _ _ _ _ _ _ _ _ _ _ because of the

   _ _ _ _ _ _ _ _ _ _ _ .

8. The tires are _ _ _ _ .

9. Mrs. Kent says she only wants a transportation car. The salesperson says, "Why didn't you

   _ _ _ _ _ ?"

●● WORK WITH A PARTNER. Some of the words below are underlined. Substitute the vocabulary words which have the same meaning as the underlined words. Then ask your partner each of the questions. When you finish, have your partner question you.

1. Do you like a large part of the car that uses energy to develop power?
   Question: Do you like a large engine?

   Answer: _____

2. How is the device that mixes gasoline spray and air to make an explosive mixture in this skit?

   Question: _____

   Answer: _____

3. Have you ever driven on smooth tires?

   Question: _____

   Answer: _____

4. What number of miles per gallon of gasoline does a good car get?

   Question: _____

   Answer: _____

35

5. Do you have a good <u>device to silence noise</u> on your car?

   Question: _____

   Answer: _____

6. Have you ever had a mechanic <u>examine and rebuild</u> your engine?

   Question: _____

   Answer: _____

7. Have you ever been to a <u>place where cars are sold</u>?

   Question: _____

   Answer: _____

8. How many miles <u>has your car been driven since it was new</u>?

   Question: _____

   Answer: _____

9. When you want something, do you <u>tell someone</u>?

   Question: _____

   Answer: _____

10. How does your car <u>work</u>?

    Question: _____

    Answer: _____

●●● NOW CHANGE PARTNERS.　Finish the following sentences using your own ideas.

1. My <u>carburetor</u> _____

2. Good <u>gas mileage</u> _____

3. <u>Bald</u> tires _____

4. A good <u>engine</u> _____

5. A good <u>muffler</u> _____

6. You need an <u>overhaul</u> when _____

7. A <u>car lot</u> _____

8. When a car <u>has 100,000 miles</u> _____

9. I <u>say so</u> when _____

10. My car <u>runs</u> _____

COMMUNICATING YOUR FEELINGS—AN EXPANSION EXERCISE

DEGREES OF INTENSITY (INFORMAL)

Average	*Intense*	*Very Intense*
Oh well. Hmmm.	That's unfortunate. a shame. too bad. *aw!*	That's terrible. awful. disgusting. horrible.

Repeat the "Degrees of Intensity" after your teacher.

WORK WITH A PARTNER. Respond to the following statements using (in your opinion) the appropriate level of intensity.

1. **Partner:** I didn't pass the test.

   You: _____

2. **Partner:** There was a murder in the neighborhood.

   You: _____

3. **Partner:** An elderly man was shot in front of his home.

   You: _____

4. **Partner:** I won't be able to go to the party with you.

   You: _____

5. **Partner:** The Mexican restaurant is closed. We'll have to go somewhere else for lunch.

   You: _____

6. **You:** My (wife/husband) and I had a fight last night.

   Partner: _____

7. **You:** I didn't get the job.

   Partner: _____

8. **You:** They raised taxes again.

   Partner: _____

9. **You:** The school will be closed for the next three days.

   Partner: _____

10. **You:** I gained five pounds.

    Partner: _____

Discuss the following questions in small groups. Choose a discussion leader to report back to the class when you finish.

1. What is your ideal car and why?

2. A person has to be careful when buying a used car in the United States. How does this compare to your native country?

3. Is it better to buy a used car from a private person or from a car lot? Why?

4. What should you do if you buy a used car and you find out it runs poorly?

5. Group activity: Write a conversation. One of your group's members is a salesperson, another is a customer, and the others are the customer's friends. The customer should tell the salesperson what type of car he is looking for. The salesperson should try to sell him the "perfect car." The following are the cars the salesperson has in the car lot.

| 1983 sports car 22 MPG[1] $30,000 | 1981 compact 35 MPG $8,000 | 1982 station wagon 22 MPG $13,000 | 1980 luxury car 13 MPG $15,000 |

[1] MPG: Miles per gallon (of gasoline).

A USED CAR

Finish writing this skit in a small group (five or more people). Try to use as many vocabulary words from the previous two skits as you can.

Props: fill in as necessary.

Scene: Harry is trying to sell his 1970 station wagon. He wants to get a good price for it because he wants to buy a new car for himself. Unfortunately, Harry's car isn't in good condition. Sometimes the car starts; sometimes it doesn't. It smokes. The radiator overheats after fifteen minutes, and it only gets ten miles per gallon (MPG).

Prospective buyer: (To Harry) Oh, what a nice-looking car! How does it run?

Harry: _____

_____: _____

_____: _____

_____: _____

_____: _____

_____: _____

_____: _____

_____: _____

_____: _____

_____: _____

_____: _____

_____: _____

_____: _____

_____: _____

COMPREHENSION

Answer the following questions with your class.

1. Describe each group's skit in your own words.

2. Which solution to the problem do you think is best? Why?

ONE STEP FURTHER

What is the "right" thing to do in each of the following situations? Why?

1. You see a hungry-looking little boy steal some food from a grocery store. You're the only one who sees him.

2. While you're shopping you find a wallet on the floor. It has a lot of money and credit cards in it. No one is around.

3. You buy several things at a department store. You notice that the salesperson didn't charge you for a large purchase.

4. You apply for a job you really want and need. The interviewer asks you if you've ever been in trouble with the police. You have, but it was five years ago.

5. There's a big test tomorrow. Your best friend calls to tell you he has a lot of family problems and he can't study. He wants to know if he can sit next to you and copy from your test.

USING VOCABULARY TO COMMUNICATE

Play The ESL Game. See page 17 for the rules.

SMALL CLUE CARDS*

Car Vocabulary 1

1. bald
2. engine
3. carburetor
4. muffler
5. gas mileage
6. to have _____ miles

Car Vocabulary 2

1. to overhaul
2. to say so
3. car lot
4. to run
5. used
6. motorcycle

Taxes 1

1. federal
2. state
3. to deduct
4. on credit
5. to figure out
6. to gross

Taxes 2

1. disability
2. union dues
3. social security
4. state
5. credit union
6. savings plan

Expressing Excitement

1. That's nice.
2. That's wonderful.
3. That's thrilling.
4. That's incredible.
5. That's exciting.
6. That's good.

Expressing Disappointment

1. Oh well.
2. That's terrible.
3. That's a shame.
4. That's too bad.
5. Hmmm.
6. That's horrible.

* *Note:* Tear out this page and cut out the clue cards.

CAR VOCABULARY 1

1. BALD
2. ENGINE
3. CARBURET-
OR
4. MUFFLER
5. GAS MILEAGE
6. TO HAVE _____
MILES

CAR VOCABULARY 2

1. TO OVERHAUL

2. TO SAY SO

3. CAR LOT

4. TO RUN

5. USED

6. MOTOR – CYCLE

TAXES 1

1. FEDERAL

2. STATE

3. TO DEDUCT

4. ON CREDIT

5. TO FIGURE OUT

6. TO GROSS

1. DISABILITY

2. UNION DUES

3. SOCIAL SECURITY

4. STATE

5. CREDIT UNION

6. SAVINGS PLAN

EXPRESSING EXCITEMENT

1. THAT'S NICE
2. THAT'S WONDERFUL
3. THAT'S THRILLING
4. THAT'S INCREDIBLE
5. THAT'S EXCITING
6. THAT'S GOOD

EXPRESSING DISAPPOINTMENT

1. OH WELL
2. THAT'S TERRIBLE
3. THAT'S A SHAME
4. THAT'S TOO BAD
5. HMMM
6. THAT'S HORRIBLE

3

Men and Women
Stumbling Through

DAYTIME DRAMA

Props: a box that can be used as a "television."

Scene: Carol and her daughter, Lisa, are watching a daytime <u>drama</u> on television.

TV character, Vickie: (Upset) *But, Elizabeth, you just found out that your aunt is actually your mother. Your first husband, Jack, who you thought was dead, is actually alive. Now you're pregnant with Jack's baby. And you're engaged to Tom, who's a homosexual. What are you going to do?*

Carol: (To Lisa) She really should have waited to get engaged.

TV character, Elizabeth: (Very upset) *I don't know. I really don't know. I thought my mother was dead and now she's alive and here in Oak Valley.* (Very seriously) *Jack doesn't know the baby is his. And he must never know!*

Lisa: What happened to Jack?

Carol: Jack had a car accident and they never found his body. He lived, but he got amnesia[1] after the accident. Now he doesn't know who Elizabeth is. Tom has been in love with Elizabeth for years. He told her they could raise the baby as their own.

TV character, Vickie: *Elizabeth, here comes Tom. I'd better go.* (She leaves.)

TV character, Tom: *Wasn't that Vickie who just left?*

TV character, Elizabeth: (Upset) *Oh Tom. I love you, but I love Jack too. My aunt . . . I mean my mother, thinks I should tell Jack everything. But, I can't.* (More upset) *And the baby! The baby must never know who its real father is!* (Firmly) *I love you. And we'll work out your problem. I know we will.* (She smiles bravely.) (A <u>commercial</u> begins.)

Carol: Why don't we watch another <u>program</u>? How about a nice <u>musical</u> or a <u>comedy</u>?

Lisa: The only musical is <u>in black and white</u>, not <u>in color</u>. (Anxiously) Anyway, it's the commercial. Could we <u>switch it</u> to <u>channel</u> 7? I want to watch a few minutes of "Dream of Life."

Carol: (Not very happy) Oh, okay. But please adjust the <u>antenna</u>.

Lisa: Okay. (She switches the channel and adjusts the <u>antenna</u>.)

---

[1] Amnesia: the inability to remember events of your life (usually caused by a powerful hit on the head).

> **"Dream of Life"**
> **character, Robert:** *But Joan, you just found out your best friend is really your mother. Your first husband is alive, but he's got amnesia. And you just married Tim! What are you going to do???*

COMPREHENSION

Answer the following questions with your class.

1. What are Carol and Lisa watching on television?
2. What is Elizabeth's "problem"?
3. What does Carol think Elizabeth should have done?
4. What happened to Jack after the accident?
5. Who does Elizabeth love?
6. What does Carol want to watch after this program?
7. What do they watch?
8. What is Joan's problem?
9. How would you have solved Elizabeth's and Joan's problems?
10. Restate the skit in your own words. Use the illustration to help you. **(Tell what happened. Example: First, Vickie summarized Elizabeth's situation. Then. . . .)**

USING VOCABULARY TO COMMUNICATE

drama (*adj.*: dramatic)	commercial
comedy	antenna
musical	to switch (the channel)
channel	in color
program	in black and white

● WORK WITH A PARTNER. Use all ten vocabulary words and expressions from above. Fill in the blanks, one letter for each blank. Make each vocabulary word agree in tense and person with its sentence. You and your partner should agree on each answer.

Carol and Lisa were watching a __ __ __ __ __ __ __ on television. It was a daytime

__ __ __ __ __ . After watching a daytime __ __ __ __ __ , it's good to watch a

__ __ __ __ __ __ __ __ or a __ __ __ __ __ __ __ .

When the __ __ __ __ __ __ __ __ __ __ __ began, Lisa wanted __ __

__ __ __ __ __ __ the __ __ __ __ __ __ __ . Lisa told Carol that her

__ __ __ __ __ __ __ was __ __ __ __ __ __ __ __ __ __ __

__ __ __ __ __ , not __ __ __ __ __ __ __ . They decided to watch Lisa's

__ __ __ __ __ __ __ . She __ __ __ __ __ __ __ __ __ __ __ __

__ __ __ __ __ __ __ and adjusted the __ __ __ __ __ __ __ .

●● WORK WITH A PARTNER. Some of the words below are underlined. Substitute the vocabulary words which have the same meaning as the underlined words. Then ask your partner each of the questions. When you finish, have your partner question you.

52

1. Do you prefer serious shows or funny shows?

    Question: _____

    Answer: _____

2. Do you like shows with music?

    Question: _____

    Answer: _____

3. How many stations do you receive in your area?

    Question: _____

    Answer: _____

4. What is your favorite show?

    Question: _____

    Answer: _____

5. Do you have a remote control device to change the channels?

    Question: _____

    Answer: _____

6. What is your favorite advertisement on television?

    Question: _____

    Answer: _____

7. Do you have an on top of your television or on top of your roof?

    Question: _____

    Answer: _____

8. What programs do you prefer to watch in color?

    Answer: _____

9. What programs do you prefer to watch in black and white?

    Answer: _____

●●● NOW CHANGE PARTNERS. Finish the following sentences using your own ideas.

1. Daytime dramas _____ .

2. The best comedy _____ .

3. The best musical _____ .

4. The worst program on television _____ .

5. The worst channel _____ .

6. I switch the channel _____ .

7. Commercials are generally _____ .

8. A good antenna _____ .

9. Programs in color _____ .

10. Programs in black and white _____ .

COMMUNICATING YOUR FEELINGS—AN EXPANSION EXERCISE

DEGREES OF INTENSITY (INFORMAL)

Average	Intense	Very Intense
hot	boiling	about to burn up
cold	freezing	like an ice cube
full	stuffed	about to pop
hungry	starving	dying of hunger
overweight	fat	as fat as a cow as big as a horse as big as the house
underweight	skinny	as thin as a rail a bag of bones
happy	ecstatic	on cloud nine in seventh heaven
sad	depressed	in the pits on a bummer
intelligent	brilliant	a genius a brain
not intelligent	stupid	a turkey moronic a bird brain
bad	terrible	lousy
good	great	like a million (dollars or bucks)
good (food)	delicious great	sumptuous fabulous very rich (usually desserts)
nice (a thing)	pretty	beautiful exquisite

Repeat these "Degrees of Intensity" after your teacher.

WORK WITH A PARTNER. Respond to the following statements, using (in your opinion) the appropriate level of intensity.

1. You're complimenting your partner on a wonderful dinner.

   _____ .

2. It's 104°.

   _____ .

3. It's 10° below zero.

   _____ .

4. You've just finished a nice lunch.

   _____ .

5. You've just finished an extremely big dinner.

   _____ .

6. You've just failed a test.

   _____ .

7. You've just got the best grade in the class.

   _____ .

8. You're complimenting your partner on the nice outfit he's wearing.

   _____ .

9. Your friend is 6'2" tall and weighs 150 pounds.

   _____ .

10. Your friend is 5'5" tall and weighs 160 pounds.

   _____ .

ONE STEP FURTHER

Discuss the following questions in small groups. Choose a discussion leader to report back to the class when you finish.

1. Is television educational? If so, what have you learned from watching television?
2. In the average American home, the television is on over six hours a day.[1] How many hours do you watch television?
3. Daytime drama is very popular in the United States. Do you have daytime drama in your native country? If so, how does it compare to the drama presented in this skit or on television?
4. In the United States, there are commercials about body odor, bad breath, dirty clothes, etc. Do these subjects bother you? How do these subjects compare with commercials in your native country?
5. Group activity: Write a conversation. Choose one of the following.

   a. Make a commercial. (Try to sell your product. Is it better than other products? Is it cheaper? Will your life improve if you use it? etc.)
   b. Create a new television program in which you're the star(s).

[1] *Statistical Abstracts of the U.S.* (Washington, D.C.: U.S. Dept. of Commerce, Bureau of the Census, 1978).

DO YOU TAKE THIS MAN . . .

Props: a "book" for the clergyman; a ring; a sign saying, "15 minutes later."

Scene: Today is Diana's wedding day. She is in the back of the church with the bridesmaids and ushers. The wedding is almost ready to begin.

Diana: (*To one of her four bridesmaids*) I'm so nervous. Is my veil on securely enough?

Nancy: (*She checks it.*) Yes. It's perfectly secure.
(*The music begins. The bridesmaids and ushers walk down the aisle in couples, the maid of honor and best man last. The bridesmaids stand in a line on the right side of the altar, the ushers on the left. The bridegroom is standing at the altar waiting for the bride. Finally she begins to walk down the aisle. Everyone stands. When she reaches the altar, the ceremony begins.*)

Clergyman: I am extremely happy to be here today to celebrate the marriage of Diana and Richard. . . . (*He begins the wedding ceremony.*)

(15 MINUTES LATER)

Clergyman: And now, do you, Richard, take Diana for your lawful wedded wife, in sickness and in health, till death do you part?

Richard: I do.

Clergyman: And do you, Diana, take Richard for your lawful wedded husband, in sickness and in health, till death do you part?

Diana: I do.

Clergyman: (*To Richard*) You may put the ring on her finger.
(*The best man gives Richard the ring. He puts it on the third finger of Diana's left hand.*)

Clergyman: I now pronounce you husband and wife. (*To Richard*) You may now kiss the bride. (*Richard kisses the bride; then the clergyman says to the wedding guests*) I'd like to introduce Mr. and Mrs. Thomas to you now. (*The bride and groom turn around and walk down the aisle as husband and wife.*)

COMPREHENSION

Answer the following questions with your class.

1. Why is today special for Diana?
2. Who walks down the aisle first? Last?
3. What does the clergyman ask Richard?
4. Where does Richard get the ring? Where does he put it?
5. Restate the skit in your own words. Use the illustration to help you.
   (Tell what happened. Example: First the music began. Then. . . .)

USING VOCABULARY TO COMMUNICATE

bridesmaids	maid of honor
ushers	bridegroom (groom)
veil	bride
aisle	altar
best man	clergyman

● **WORK WITH A PARTNER.** Use all ten vocabulary words from above. Fill in the blanks, one letter for each blank. Make each vocabulary word agree in tense and person with its sentence. You and your partner should agree on each answer.

1. Diana was the __ __ __ __ __ . She wore a wedding dress and a __ __ __ __ .

2. Richard was the __ __ __ __ __ __ __ __ __ __ .

3. Diana had four __ __ __ __ __ __ __ __ __ __ __ .

4. The __ __ __ __   __ __   __ __ __ __ __ and the __ __ __ __   __ __ __

   walked down the __ __ __ __ __ last.

5. Richard had four __ __ __ __ __ __ .

6. The ceremony took place at the __ __ __ __ __ .

7. A __ __ __ __ __ __ __ __ __ performed the ceremony.

●● **WORK WITH A PARTNER.** Some of the words below are underlined. Substitute the vocabulary words which have the same meaning as the underlined words. Then ask your partner each of the questions. When you finish, have your partner question you.

1. Do <u>female friends of the bride</u> join in the ceremony in your native country?

   Question: _____

   Answer: _____

2. Do <u>male friends of the groom</u> join in the ceremony in your native country?

   Question: _____

   Answer: _____

3. Does the <u>woman who's getting married</u> wear a white dress in your native country?

Question: _____

Answer: _____

4. What does the <u>man who's getting married</u> wear?

   Question: _____

   Answer: _____

5. Is there a <u>best friend</u> who joins in the ceremony and helps the bride?

   Question: _____

   Answer: _____

6. Is there a <u>best friend</u> who joins in the ceremony and helps the groom?

   Question: _____

   Answer: _____

7. Do they all walk down a(n) <u>narrow path in the center of the church</u>?

   Question: _____

   Answer: _____

8. Does a <u>professional man representing the church</u> perform the ceremony?

   Question: _____

   Answer: _____

9. Does the bride wear (a) <u>something over her face</u> in your native country?

   Question: _____

   Answer: _____

10. Do the bride, groom, bridesmaids, and ushers participate in the ceremony at the <u>front of the church</u>?

   Question: _____

   Answer: _____

●●● NOW CHANGE PARTNERS. Finish the following sentences, using your own ideas.

1. A <u>bride</u> is _____ .

2. A <u>groom</u> _____ .

3. <u>Veils</u> _____ .

4. The <u>ushers</u> _____ .

5. _____ the <u>aisle</u>.

6. The <u>best man</u> _____ .

7. The <u>maid of honor</u> _____ .

8. _____ the <u>altar</u>.

9. A clergyman _____ .

10. The bridesmaids _____ .

COMMUNICATING YOUR FEELINGS—AN EXPANSION EXERCISE

DEGREES OF INTENSITY

Average	Intense	Very Intense
happy	certainly happy surely very	entirely happy completely perfectly thoroughly extremely absolutely
tired	particularly tired especially very	too tired (to do something)
enough (food for everyone)	plenty (of food)	too much (food) (more than necessary; an excessive amount)
kind of (prepared for a sort of test) somewhat	almost (prepared) nearly practically just about	completely (prepared)

Repeat these "Degrees of Intensity" after your teacher.

WORK WITH A PARTNER. Respond to the following statements, using (in your opinion) the appropriate level of intensity.

1. Your partner has been up all night studying.

2. Your partner has been up all night at a party. He can't go to school the next day.

3. Your partner just got married.

4. Your partner just finished exercising.

5. Your partner isn't quite finished washing the car.

6. Someone just gave your partner a lot of money for her birthday.

7. Your partner wants to buy a very expensive car. It costs $15,000. He doesn't have $15,000.

8. Your partner just got a good grade on a test.

9. Your partner bought four hamburgers for four people.

10. Your partner bought seven hamburgers for four people.

Discuss the following questions in small groups. Choose a discussion leader to report back to the class when you finish.

1. Describe the wedding ceremony in your native country. (Is it expensive? Do you have it in a church or temple? Are there bridesmaids? Ushers?) If possible, role-play the ceremony.

2. How old should a person be to get married? Why?

3. Which do you think is more important in a marriage; love or friendship? Why?

4. Your daughter or son comes home and says, "I'm getting married." What questions do you ask about your future son-in-law or daughter-in-law?

5. Group activity: Choose one of the following.

   a. Many American newspapers have "Personal" advertisements. A lonely man or woman can advertise to find a mate.[1] Make an advertisement for a mate. First, find someone in your group who wants a mate. Tell what kind of mate he's looking for. The example will help you.

   Example: | Single man, 27, 5'11", 160 lbs., nice looking, successful. Interested in sports, movies, and music. Wants attractive woman from 18 to 24 with similar interests for friendship. Photo appreciated.

   b. Write a conversation which shows Diana and Richard's relationship in twenty-five years. (Do they have children? Are they getting along well? etc.)

---

[1] The majority of people don't advertise for a mate. If a person does this, he must be very careful.

TWO VIEWS OF MARRIAGE—REVIEW

Work in a small group (five or more people). Write the lines for one view of marriage. You can show what you think marriage is or what you think it should be.

Props: fill in as necessary.

Scene #1: Tom works in an office. He comes home after a hard day. He is greeted by his wife, Alice, and their two children.

Tom: (*Calling*) I'm home!

Alice: _____

____ : _____

____ : _____

____ : _____

____ : _____

____ : _____

____ : _____

____ : _____

_____
_____
_____

Scene #2: Linda works in an office. She comes home after a hard day. She is greeted by her husband, John, and their two children.

Linda: (*Calling*) I'm home!

John: _____

____ : _____

____ : _____

____ : _____

____ : _____

____ : _____

____ : _____

COMPREHENSION

Answer the following questions with your class.

1. Describe each view of marriage 1.

2. Describe each view of marriage 2.

3. Are any of these views similar to marriage in your native country? Different? In what ways?

4. What do you think marriage is really like?

5. What do you want marriage to be like?

ONE STEP FURTHER

Discuss the following questions in small groups. Choose a discussion leader to report back to the class when you finish.

1. In most cultures there is a lot of preparation for the wedding but little preparation for the life that follows. How can you prepare yourself for marriage?

2. What do you think about living together before marriage? Why? Is this possible in your native country?

3. Do children change a marriage? If so, in what ways?

4. Some people don't feel they have to get married. They stay single a lifetime. Do you have a choice in your native country whether to get married or not?

5. Is marriage necessary to a culture? If so, why? If not, why not?

USING VOCABULARY TO COMMUNICATE

Play The ESL Game. See page 17 for the rules.

SMALL CLUE CARDS*

Television 1	*Television 2*
1. channel	1. program
2. commercial	2. antenna
3. drama	3. in color
4. comedy	4. in black and white
5. musical	5. to watch
6. to switch	6. to switch

Wedding 1	*Wedding 2*
1. maid of honor	1. bride
2. best man	2. bridesmaids
3. veil	3. ushers
4. altar	4. groom
5. aisle	5. ring
6. ceremony	6. clergyman

Degrees of Intensity 1	*Degrees of Intensity 2*
1. about to burn up	1. happy
2. hungry	2. plenty
3. as fat as a cow	3. too much
4. on cloud nine	4. very tired
5. delicious	5. very happy
6. a genius	6. extremely happy

*Note: Tear out this page and cut out the clue cards.

1. CHANNEL

2. COMMERCIAL

3. DRAMA

4. COMEDY

5. MUSICAL

6. TO SWITCH

1. PROGRAM

2. ANTENNA

3. IN COLOR

4. IN BLACK AND WHITE

5. TO WATCH

6. TO SWITCH

1. MAID OF HONOR

2. BEST MAN

3. VEIL

4. ALTAR

5. AISLE

6. CEREMONY

WEDDING 2

1. **BRIDE**

2. **BRIDES-MAIDS**

3. **USHERS**

4. **GROOM**

5. **RING**

6. **CLERGYMAN**

DEGREES OF INTENSITY 1

1. **ABOUT TO BURN UP**

2. **HUNGRY**

3. **AS FAT AS A COW**

4. **ON CLOUD NINE**

5. **DELICIOUS**

6. **A GENIUS**

1. HAPPY

2. PLENTY

3. TOO MUCH

4. VERY TIRED

5. VERY HAPPY

6. EXTREMELY HAPPY

4

Impressions
and Values

A Mystery
UFO
The Fountain—Review

A MYSTERY

Props: a hat and an eyeglass for the detective.

Scene: José Carlos Ruiz de la Torre is a <u>private detective.</u> Kanako Kiyohara hired him to find out who killed her boyfriend, Benjamin.

Kanako: (*Pacing back and forth[1] and crying occasionally*) Where's that detective? We can't <u>wait</u> <u>for</u> him much longer.

Sandy: (*Gently*) Don't worry. We'll <u>find out</u> who killed Benjamin. Don't worry.

John: Yeah. A man like that should be in jail.

Steve: Who said it was a man? (*He looks at John suspiciously.*)
(*No one notices José, who's been looking at each suspect[2] thoroughly.*)

José: Hello. I'm José Carlos Ruiz de la Torre. You can call me Joe.

Kanako: (Crying) I'm . . . I'm . . . (*Crying harder*) I'm Benjamin's girlfriend.

José: Yes. (*He <u>looks at</u> Kanako suspiciously.*) Is it true that you and Steve are dating?

Kanako: (*Innocently*) Yes. We <u>go out</u> occasionally, but we're just friends. Really.

José: (*To Steve*) Is it true that you gave Kanako an engagement ring[3] last night?

Steve: (*Innocently*) Well, yes.
(*José walks over to Sandy.*)

José: (*To Sandy*) Is it true that you wrote a love poem[4] to Benjamin the day before he died?

Sandy: (*Yelling*) Yes! Yes, it's true! (*She points to Kanako.*) I loved him more than she did! Yes, yes, yes!

Kanako: (*Hurt*) Sandy.

José: (To John) Is it true that you and Benjamin both <u>applied for</u> the same job?

John: (*Innocently*) Sure. So what?

---

[1] Pacing back and forth: walking back and forth nervously.

[2] Suspect: a person who might have committed a crime (killed Benjamin).

[3] Engagement ring: a ring a man gives a woman as a promise of marriage (usually a diamond).

[4] Poem: a special arrangement of words expressing ideas or feelings more powerfully than usual (poems often rhyme).

José: Is it true that Benjamin got the job?

John: Benjamin got everything. (*Yelling*) I hated him!

Steve: I hated him too. He wouldn't let Kanako go.

Sandy: (*Sadly*) I loved him, (*softly*) but he didn't love me.

José: (*Excited*) I've got it! I know who shot Benjamin!

(*The lights go out. Everyone screams. When the lights go on we see that José is on the floor. He's been shot. His last words are, "It's. . . ."*)

COMPREHENSION

Answer the following questions with your class.

1. What does José Carlos Ruiz de la Torre do?
2. Why did Kanako hire him?
3. Why do you think Steve is suspicious of John?
4. Do you think Kanako loved Benjamin? Explain.
5. How do you think Sandy felt about Benjamin?
6. How do you think Sandy feels about Kanako?
7. Why do you think John hated Benjamin?
8. Who do you think killed Benjamin? Why?
9. Who do you think killed José? Why?
10. Restate the skit in your own words. Use the illustration to help you. **(Tell what happened. Example: Kanako, Sandy, John, and Steve were talking about Benjamin's killer. José introduced himself. . . .)**

USING VOCABULARY TO COMMUNICATE

Two-Word Verbs

hurt
excited
private
detective
mystery

wait for
find out
apply for
look at
go out (with someone)

- WORK WITH A PARTNER. Use vocabulary words from above. Fill in the blanks, one letter for each blank. Make each vocabulary word agree in tense and person with its sentence. You and your partner should agree on each answer.

1. José Carlos Ruiz de la Torre is a __ __ __ __ __ __ __   __ __ __ __ __ __ __ __ __ __ .

2. Kanako hired him to solve a __ __ __ __ __ __ __ .

3. Sandy said she loved Benjamin. Kanako was __ __ __ __ .

4. José became __ __ __ __ __ __ __ . He knew who shot Benjamin.

WORK WITH A PARTNER. Some of the words below are underlined. Substitute the vocabulary words which have the same meaning as the underlined words. Then ask your partner each of the questions. When you finish, have your partner question you.

1. Are you <u>awaiting</u> any interesting news?

   Question: _____

   Answer: _____

2. Who is your best friend <u>dating</u>?

   Question: _____

   Answer: _____

3. What do you enjoy <u>watching</u> when you're in a strange city?

   Question: _____

   Answer: _____

4. Have you ever <u>formally requested</u> a job?

   Question: _____

   Answer: _____

5. What is the most interesting secret you've ever <u>discovered</u>?

   Question: _____

   Answer: _____

NOW CHANGE PARTNERS. Finish the following sentences using your own ideas.

1. My partner felt <u>hurt</u> when _____ .

2. My partner is <u>excited</u> because _____ .

3. A <u>detective</u> _____ .

4. A <u>private</u> detective _____ .

5. A <u>mystery</u> _____ .

6. I hate <u>waiting for</u> _____ .

7. Last week I <u>found out</u> _____ .

8. My partner often <u>goes out</u> _____ .

9. I love looking at _____ .

10. I want to apply for _____ .

COMMUNICATING YOUR FEELINGS—AN EXPANSION EXERCISE

RESPONDING TO INVITATIONS

| | YES | | NO | |
	Average	Strong	Average	Strong
INFORMAL	Do you want to see a movie? Okay. Sure, why not? Yeah.	Do you want to see a movie? Okay, let's do it. I sure do. Yeah, let's go.	Do you want to see a movie? Not really, thanks. Not this time, thanks.	Do you want to see a movie? No thanks.
FORMAL	Would you like to see a movie? Yes, I would.	Would you like to see a movie? I'd love it. I'd be delighted.	Would you like to see a movie? I'm sorry, but I'm busy.	Would you like to see a movie? No, thank you.

Repeat the above after your teacher.

WORK WITH A PARTNER.   Respond to the following invitations, using (in your opinion) the appropriate level of intensity.

1. **Partner:** Would you like to go to the museum?

    You: _____

2. **Partner:** Do you want to go to a free rock concert tonight?

    You: _____

3. **You:** Do you want to study together tonight?

    Partner: _____

4. **You:** Would you like to go swimming?

    Partner: _____

5. **Partner:** Do you want to go to Hawaii?

    You: _____

ONE STEP FURTHER

Discuss the following questions in small groups. Choose a discussion leader to report back to the class when you finish.

1. Do you think most people present an "image"[1] to the world and keep their real feelings hidden? Explain. Describe some of the "images" the characters in the skit presented.

2. What do you think your "image" is? Is it different at different times? With different people? Describe

    a. Your parents' image of you.
    b. Your spouse's[2] (or friend's) image of you.
    c. Your classmates' image of you.
    d. Your teacher's image of you.
    e. Your image of yourself.

3. Do you think it's possible for someone to know what you really think and how you really feel? How many people really know you?

4. Do "clothes make the man"? What does this phrase mean? How much effect do your clothes have on you? How do you feel in formal clothes? In a bathing suit? In jeans? In a business suit? How do you feel when you're dressed too formally or informally for an occasion?

5. Group activity: Choose a member of your group who wants to be a politician. Create an "image" for him or her. Include the type of clothing he or she will wear, the things he or she will believe in, the type of people he or she will represent, etc.

---

[1] Image: impression; the way people see you; appearance. (Your image is the way other people see you.)
[2] Spouse: husband or wife.

UFO[1]

Props: toy guns, if possible.

Scene: A UFO lands on earth. The passengers, Mork, Ork, Cork, and Dork, get out of their spaceship and observe earth for the first time.

Mork: (*Looking around*) Strange. Very strange.

Cork: What's strange?

Mork: There are so many children. They tell the adults where to go next and what to do. Children must rule this planet.

Ork: (*He points to a line of people standing outside a small fragile-looking building.*) Why is everyone standing still?

Mork: They stand in long lines for hours. Finally, they give a young lady a small piece of paper. She lets a few people get into cars with no tops.

Dork: What do the cars do inside the building?

Mork: Someone drives the cars in circles in the dark and the people sit there screaming.

Cork: (*Scratching his head*) Very interesting.

Ork: (*He points to a tall fat man with painted eyes and lips who's surrounded by children.*) Look how they admire him. He must be a God!

Mork: (*Screaming*) Look out! Everybody get down! (*They all hide behind a table.*)

Ork: (*He gets up.*) It's okay now. Two men were having a gunfight. One shot the other. When the man who was hit fell down, I thought he was dead. Then he got up and smiled at me. Their bodies must be very strong.
(*They walk past the saloon and see some boats.*)

Cork: Let's get on this boat. I'd like to go to another part of the planet.
(*They all board a two-level steamer.*)

(FIVE MINUTES LATER)

Mork: Look! It's stopping! We're back at the same place we started!

Dork: Strange transportation system.

---

[1] UFO: Unidentified flying object (something from another planet).

Cork: What's this section of the planet called anyway?

Mork: I'll check. (*He points to a sign.*) I see a big sign over there. It says "Disneyland."

COMPREHENSION

Answer the following questions with your class.

1. What lands on earth? Who are the passengers?
2. Who does Mork think rules earth? Why?
3. Why do the people stand in lines for so long? What does Cork think about this?
4. What do you think the tall, fat man with painted eyes and lips is? What does Ork think he is?
5. Why does Mork tell everyone to get down?
6. What happened in the saloon?
7. Why do they board a boat?
8. Why do you think the boat took them back to where they started?
9. Where are they?
10. Restate the skit in your own words. Use the illustration to help you. **(Tell what happened. Example: Mork, Cork, Ork, and Dork landed on earth. . . .)**

USING VOCABULARY TO COMMUNICATE

- WORK WITH A PARTNER. Match the vocabulary words on the left with their meanings on the right. There are more definitions than vocabulary words. You and your partner should agree on each answer.

___c___	1. **earth**	a. to see; to take notice of
_____	2. **spaceship**	b. to recognize
_____	3. **to observe**	c. the planet that we live on
_____	4. **to rule**	d. soft
_____	5. **planet**	e. hard
_____	6. **fragile**	f. a public bar (term used for bars in the American West, nineteenth century)
_____	7. **to admire**	g. a ship for travel between planets
_____	8. **saloon**	h. an airplane
_____	9. **to board**	i. a boat powered by steam
_____	10. **steamer**	j. to govern; to control
		k. to look up to; to regard highly
		l. heavenly body that revolves around the sun (Mars, Mercury, Earth)
		m. to get on a ship (boat, airplane)
		n. weak; easily broken

Together, rearrange the following words to make sentences in English. Follow the example.

Example: Friday graduation next is
Next Friday is graduation.

1. UFO earth a landed on

_____

2. observe the it for time passengers sent the were to first

_____

3. a came spaceship they in

_____

4. planet children thought Mork ruled the

_____

5. buildings fragile they looking observed the

_____

6. fat admired man a children tall

_____

7. in fight saloon was the a gun there

_____

8. part a another planet because wanted the of they go they to to boarded boat

_____

9. steamer was a it

_____

COMMUNICATING YOUR FEELINGS—AN EXPANSION EXERCISE

GIVING AND RECEIVING COMPLIMENTS

	Giving	*Receiving*
INFORMAL	That's a great-looking outfit. That's a sharp outfit. That's a great report. That was a great meal.	Gee, thanks. Thanks a lot. Thank you. I'm glad you liked it.
FORMAL	That's a very attractive outfit. Your report was excellent. That was a lovely meal.	Thank you. What a nice compliment! What a nice thing to say. Thank you. Thank you. I'm glad you enjoyed it.

Repeat the above after your teacher.

WORK WITH A PARTNER. Compliment your partner and have him respond appropriately.

1. Compliment your partner on his car.

    You: _____

    Partner: _____

2. Compliment your partner on his most recent test score.

    You: _____

    Partner: _____

3. Compliment your partner on his smile.

    You: _____

    Partner: _____

4. Compliment your partner on his English.

    You: _____

    Partner: _____

5. Compliment your partner on his outfit.

    You: _____

    Partner: _____

ONE STEP FURTHER

Discuss the following questions in small groups. Choose a discussion leader to report back to the class when you finish.

1. Do you believe in UFOs? Why or why not?

2. Do you think man will be living on other planets by the year 2000?

3. Do you think there's life on other planets? If so, is it similar to human life or different? Do you think they are more or less advanced than we are? Do they speak English?

4. If you could go to another planet, would you? Why or why not?

5. Group activity: When we speak of different countries, we separate people. (Example: You're Japanese, Chinese, American, etc.) When we speak of different planets, we unify people. (Example: You're from earth.) Make a list of things that make people the same regardless of their birthplace. Possible examples include:

    a. Desire to have children   h.
    b. Need for food   i.
    c.   j.
    d.   k.
    e.   l.
    f.   m.
    g.   n.

THE FOUNTAIN—REVIEW

Finish writing this skit in a small group (five or more people). Try to use as many vocabulary words from the previous two skits as you can.

Props: fill in as necessary.

Scene: Your friend, who's a scientist, has just discovered a pill that can give eternal[1] youth. The only problem is he only has two pills and he can't make any more.

Scientist: I've just discovered a pill that can give eternal youth! (*Sadly*) But I only have two pills.

Ponsa: (*Excited*) Well, let's take them!

Scientist: But we could give them to a president or a king or the Pope!

Ponsa: _____

_____: _____

_____: _____

_____: _____

_____: _____

_____: _____

_____: _____

_____: _____

_____: _____

_____: _____

_____: _____

_____: _____

[1] Eternal: forever.

COMPREHENSION

Answer the following questions with your class.

1. Describe each group's solution to the problem.

2. Which solution do you think is best? Why?

ONE STEP FURTHER

Discuss the following questions in small groups. Choose a discussion leader to report back to the class when you finish.

1. What is old age? Does it have more to do with the number of years you've lived or your mental and physical condition? Can you be old at twenty-five and young at fifty? Explain.

2. Do you think that man will be able to live forever someday? If someone offered you eternal youth, would you want it? Why or why not?

3. Americans are very youth-oriented. They spend millions of dollars on cosmetics, vitamins, and other products to slow the effects of aging. What do you think about this? How does it compare to your native country? Is it okay to wrinkle and grow old? Why do you think Americans fight it so much?

4. Many people have plastic surgery[1] to improve their appearances or to stop the effects of aging. Would you ever have plastic surgery? Do you think it's okay for other people to have it? Why or why not?

5. Group activity: Role-play or describe yourself physically and mentally at age sixty. (You can role-play with a spouse, friend, etc.)

USING VOCABULARY TO COMMUNICATE

Play The ESL Game. See page 17 for the rules.

---

[1] Plastic surgery: cosmetic surgery (surgery to improve your appearance).

SMALL CLUE CARDS*

Mystery—Easy Vocabulary

1. to kill
2. jail
3. girlfriend
4. love
5. job
6. thorough

UFO—Easy Vocabulary

1. to scream
2. strange
3. cars
4. to shoot
5. boat
6. sign

UFO 1

1. to observe
2. to rule
3. fragile
4. saloon
5. steamer
6. to board

UFO 2

1. earth
2. planet
3. spaceship
4. to board
5. the sun
6. to admire

Two-Word Verbs +1

1. wait for
2. find out
3. apply for
4. look at
5. go out
6. look for

A Mystery

1. hurt
2. excited
3. detective
4. private
5. mystery
6. engagement ring

Note: +1 means that an additional word was taken from the skit that was not necessarily practiced as a vocabulary word.

*Note: Tear out this page and cut out the clue cards.

MYSTERY—EASY VOCABULARY

1. TO KILL

2. JAIL

3. GIRLFRIEND

4. LOVE

5. JOB

6. THOROUGH

UFO—EASY VOCABULARY

1. TO SCREAM

2. STRANGE

3. CARS

4. TO SHOOT

5. BOAT

6. SIGN

1. **TO OBSERVE**

2. **TO RULE**

3. **FRAGILE**

4. **SALOON**

5. **STEAMER**

6. **TO BOARD**

1. EARTH

2. PLANET

3. SPACESHIP

4. TO BOARD

5. THE SUN

6. TO ADMIRE

1. WAIT FOR

2. FIND OUT

3. APPLY FOR

4. LOOK AT

5. GO OUT

6. LOOK FOR

A MYSTERY

1. HURT

2. EXCITED

3. DETECTIVE

4. PRIVATE

5. MYSTERY

6. ENGAGEMENT RING

5

Employment

DON'T CALL US, WE'LL CALL YOU—PART 1

Props: gum, a cup for coffee, a jacket, a tie, and cigarettes.

Scene: Michael had a job interview at 2:30 P.M. His car wouldn't start. He had to walk two miles in 101° weather to the interview. He was thirty minutes late.

Michael: (*Wiping his forehead*) What a hot day! (*He takes out some gum and starts chewing it.*) Ah! That's better.

Secretary: May I help you?

Michael: I hope so. (*He puts his jacket and tie on a chair.*) I have an appointment with the personnel manager.

Secretary: Oh yes. You must be the young man who just graduated from college. I've heard nice things about you. May I have your résumé and three letters of recommendation?

Michael: Oh no! I left them in the car!
(*The personnel manager comes out.*)

Personnel Manager: (*To the secretary*) Is my next interview here yet?

Secretary: Yes. (*The personnel manager goes back into her office.*) (*To Michael*) You can go in now.

Michael: (*He throws away his gum, puts on his jacket, straightens his tie, walks into the office, and trips over the rug. He tries to shake hands with the personnel manager, but spills a cup of coffee all over her desk instead.*) Oh! I'm very sorry!

Manager: It's okay. My desk was dirty anyway. (*Changing the subject*) First of all, what are your qualifications?

Michael: (*Lighting a cigarette*) Well, I just graduated from college so I don't have any work experience. I majored in psychology.

Manager: Well, that's good. (*Looking at his cigarette*) We need two full-time counselors and one part-time counselor.

Michael: The part-time position[1] would be better for me. I like to have a lot of free time. (*Puffing on his cigarette*) What do your counselors do?

Manager: They help people quit smoking.

[1] Position: job.

Michael: Oh. (*He puts out his cigarette.*)

Manager: Do you have any other questions?

Michael: Yeah. Do you pay well?

Manager: Salaries are based on experience.

Michael: What are the <u>benefits</u>?

Manager: We have a complete medical and dental plan. We give a one-week vacation the first year and a two-week vacation the second year. Do you have any other questions?

Michael: Nope.[2]

Manager: We have your <u>application</u> on file. We'll call you when we finish interviewing the other applicants. (*She stands.*)

Michael: (*He stands.*) Thanks a lot. 'Bye.

Manager: Good-bye.

Now go on to DON'T CALL US, WE'LL CALL YOU—PART 2.

---

[2] Nope: no (very informal).

DON'T CALL US, WE'LL CALL YOU—PART 2

Props: a résumé, three letters of recommendation.

Scene: Kahlil has a job interview at 2:30 P.M. He arrives at the interview ten minutes early. He's wearing a nice suit.

Kahlil: (*To the secretary*) Hello. My name is Kahlil Jabrin. I have an <u>interview</u> at 2:30 P.M. with the <u>personnel manager</u>.

Secretary: Oh yes. I've heard nice things about you. May I have your <u>résumé</u> and three <u>letters of recommendation?</u>

Kahlil: Certainly. (*He hands her the résumé and letters.*)
(*The personnel manager comes out.*)

Personnel Manager: (*To the secretary*) I'm ready for my next <u>interview</u> now. Do you have the résumé?

Secretary: Yes. Right here. (*She hands her the résumé and letters of recommendation.*) (*To Kahlil*) You can go in now.

Kahlil: (*He walks up to the personnel manager and waits for her to offer her hand. She does.*) I'm Kahlil Jabrin. It's very nice to meet you.

Manager: It's nice to meet you, too. Please have a seat. (*She looks at Kahlil's résumé and letters of recommendation.*) These are very impressive.

Kahlil: Thank you. I enjoy working with people very much.

Manager: (*Looking at the résumé*) It says that you worked as a <u>part-time</u> summer counselor. Tell me about that job.

Kahlil: It was very similar to what you do here. We helped teenagers quit smoking.

Manager: Very interesting. Do you have any questions?

Kahlil: Yes. I'd like to know what method you use to help people quit smoking.

Manager: We have a book that explains our method. You can get the book from our secretary.

Kahlil: Thank you. I'd be very interested in reading it.

Manager: We have medical and dental <u>benefits</u> and a one-week vacation the first year and a two-week vacation the second year. We do require some <u>overtime</u> occasionally. I hope that's not a problem.

Kahlil: No. That's fine.

Manager: (*She stands.*) We have a few more <u>applicants</u> to interview, but we will call you soon.

Kahlil: (*He stands.*) Thank you very much for your time. (*They shake hands.*) Good-bye.

Manager: Good-bye.

COMPREHENSION

Answer the following questions with your class.

Part 1

1. Why does Michael walk to the interview?
2. Why do you think he puts his jacket and tie on the chair?
3. Where are his résumé and letters of recommendation?
4. What happens when he walks into the personnel manager's office?
5. Why did Michael put out his cigarette?
6. What do you think he did wrong?
7. Do you think he got the job? Why or why not?
8. Restate the skit in your own words. Use the illustration to help you. (**Tell what happened. Example: First, Michael was late for the interview, etc.**)

Part 2

1. What time is it when Kahlil arrives at the interview?
2. What does he bring with him?
3. Does he have any experience? If so, what?
4. What questions does he ask?
5. What did he do right?
6. Do you think he got the job? Why or why not?
7. Restate the skit in your own words. Use the illustration to help you. (**Tell what happened. Example: First, Kahlil introduced himself, etc.**)

USING VOCABULARY TO COMMUNICATE

interview
personnel manager
résumé
overtime
letters of recommendation

qualifications
benefits
application (applicant)
full-time
part-time

● WORK WITH A PARTNER. Use all ten vocabulary words from above. Fill in the blanks, one letter for each blank. Make each vocabulary word agree in tense and person with its sentence. You and your partner should agree on each answer.

1. Both Kahlil and Michael had __ __ __ __ __ __ __ __ __ __ __ with the

   __ __ __ __ __ __ __ __ __   __ __ __ __ __ __ __ __ .

2. Kahlil brought his __ __ __ __ __ __ and three __ __ __ __ __ __ __

   __ __   __ __ __ __ __ __ __ __ __ __ __ __ __ .

3. The __ __ __ __ __ __ __ __ __ __   __ __ __ __ __ __ __ asked Michael about his

   __ __ __ __ __ __ __ __ __ __ __ __ __ __ .

4. Michael wanted to work __ __ __ __   __ __ __ __ , not __ __ __ __

   __ __ __ __ .

5. Michael probably wouldn't want to work __ __ __ __ __ __ __ __ .

6. The __ __ __ __ __ __ __ __ included a full medical and dental plan.

7. All __ __ __ __ __ __ __ __ __ __ have to fill out an

   __ __ __ __ __ __ __ __ __ __ __ .

●● WORK WITH A PARTNER. Use the clues below to fill in the puzzle on the next page.

Across

1. References from past employers or teachers. These letters tell what a good employee you'd be.
5. A written summary of job experience and education. You include the information you want. You make your own ____ .
8. When a worker works full-time, he often receives more than a salary or an hourly wage. He may get medical insurance, dental insurance, vacations, etc.
9. Special abilities
10. A written request for a job. The company gives you a blank ____ to fill out with the information they request.

Down

2. "I'll only work eight hours a day. I don't like to work ____ ."
3. This person supervises the hiring and training of employees.
4. An appointment with an employer to try to get a job.
6. Eight hours a day, five days a week
7. Fewer than eight hours a day or fewer than five days a week

●●● NOW CHANGE PARTNERS. Finish the following sentences, using your own ideas.

1. The last <u>interview</u> I had was _____ .

2. A <u>personnel manager</u> _____ .

3. A good <u>résumé</u> _____ .

4. My <u>qualifications</u> are _____ .

5. <u>Part-time</u> work _____ .

6. <u>Full-time</u> work _____ .

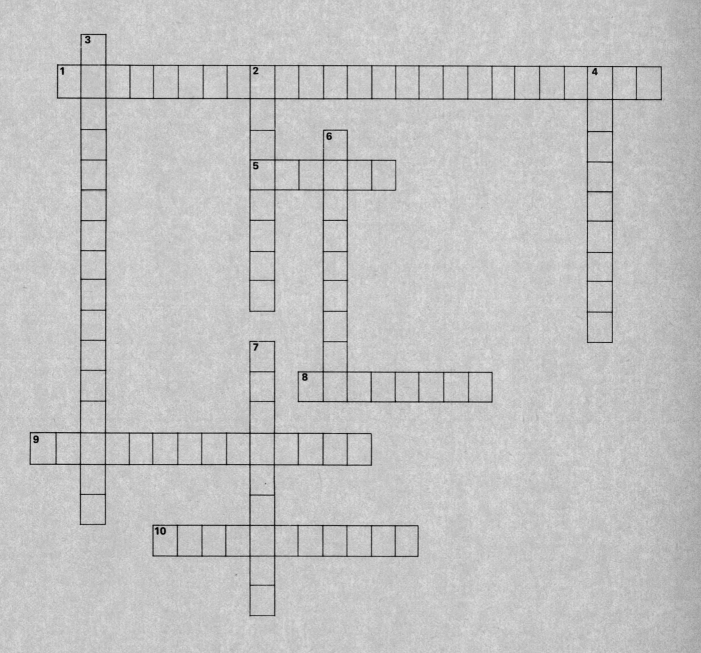

7. Good <u>benefits</u> include _____.

8. The last <u>application</u> I filled out was for _____.

9. I _____ <u>overtime</u>.

10. Good <u>letters of recommendation</u> include _____.

COMMUNICATING YOUR FEELINGS

EXPRESSING DISSATISFACTION

	Average	*Strong*
TO A NEIGHBOR	I hate to complain but I've got a big test tommorrow. Could you turn your radio down?	I'd appreciate it if you could turn your radio down.
TO A REPAIRPERSON	My _____ doesn't seem to be working properly. Could you please check it?	My _____ doesn't work at all. When is the soonest you can check it?
IN A RESTAURANT	Excuse me. I ordered a rare steak and this one is well done. Could you please take it back?	Excuse me. I ordered a rare steak and this one is well done. I'd like to send it back.
TO A SALESPERSON	This merchandise doesn't seem to be working properly. I wonder if I could exchange it.	This merchandise is defective. I'd like to exchange it.

Repeat the above after your teacher.

WORK WITH A PARTNER. Respond to the following complaints, using (in your opinion) the appropriate level of intensity.

1. Complain about sour milk in a restaurant.

   Partner: _____

   You: _____

2. Complain about your _____ that was fixed three times but is still broken.
   (appliance)

   Partner: _____

   You: _____

3. Complain about the lights being out in your parking lot.

   Partner: _____

   You: _____

4. Complain about your neighbor's loud parties.

   Partner: _____

   You: _____

5. Complain about the mechanic postponing the repair of your car.

Partner: _____

You: _____

ONE STEP FURTHER

Discuss the following questions in small groups. Choose a discussion leader to report back to the class when you finish.

1. Is it possible to be relaxed for a job interview? How?

2. Assume you just graduated from high school. You're planning to go to college in one year. You interview for a permanent full-time job that you need very badly. Do you explain your plans to your interviewers? If they ask if you're going to stay at the job permanently, what do you say?

3. A few minutes can affect you for years. How can you do your best at job interviews and other important meetings?

4. You have interviews for two jobs. You really want the second job, but you've heard nothing from the interviewer. You receive a letter offering you the first job. What do you do?

5. Group activity: The following are suggestions for a job interview:

   a. Be on time.
   b. Find out if you need to bring anything with you before the interview (résumé, letters of recommendation, etc.).
   c. Speak clearly.
   d. Be polite.
   e. Dress well, but conservatively.
   f. Don't smoke or chew gum.
   g. Think before you answer the interviewer's questions.
   h. Express a sincere interest in the job.
   i. Try to get information about the job and company before the interview.
   j. Thank the interviewer for her time.

   The following are questions an interviewer might ask:
   a. What are your qualifications (education, job experience)?
   b. Have you ever done a job like this before?
   c. Can you work overtime?
   d. Why did you leave your last job?
   e. Why do you want this job?
   f. Do you plan to stay permanently?
   Now role-play an interview for a job you would like. Take turns being the job applicant and the interviewer. When you finish, have the group evaluate each interview. Did each applicant get the job? Why or why not?

THE PERFECT EMPLOYEE—REVIEW

Finish writing this skit in a small group (five or more people). Try to use as many vocabulary words from the previous two skits as you can.

Props: fill in as necessary.

Scene: Dennis is at work. It is 6:00 P.M. on Friday night. Dennis has to catch a plane for New York to help plan a surprise party for his parents' fiftieth wedding anniversary. The party will be on Saturday night.

Boss: Dennis, I'd like to talk to you for a minute.

Dennis: (*Straightening the papers on his desk*) Yes?

Boss: We have a very important job that has to be finished before Monday. Can you work this weekend?

Dennis: _____

_____: _____

_____: _____

_____: _____

_____: _____

_____: _____

_____: _____

_____: _____

_____: _____

_____: _____

_____: _____

_____: _____

COMPREHENSION

Answer the following questions with your class.

1. Describe each group's skit in your own words.
2. Which solution to the problem do you think is best? Why?

ONE STEP FURTHER

Discuss the following questions in small groups. Choose a discussion leader to report back to the class when you finish.

1. What should you do if your boss doesn't like you?

2. What should you do if you don't like your boss?

3. Is it necessary to like your co-workers?

4. Group activity: Your group should find a solution to one of the following problems.

   a. You do work that a co-worker takes credit for.
      OR
   b. You work with someone who is not doing his job well. You've been "helping" this person by staying late to finish his work. Now you don't have enough time to do your own work.

5. Group activity: List ten (or more) qualities for the perfect employee. List them in their order of importance. (The most important quality should be first; the least important, last.) The first two qualities are suggestions to get you started.

   1. Experience
   2. Punctuality
   3.
   4.
   5.
   6.
   7.
   8.
   9.
   10.

USING VOCABULARY TO COMMUNICATE

Play The ESL Game. See page 17 for the rules.

SMALL CLUE CARDS*

Job Vocabulary 1
1. interview
2. personnel manager
3. qualifications
4. benefits
5. resume
6. application

Job Vocabulary 2
1. resume
2. overtime
3. full-time
4. letters of recommendation
5. part-time
6. interview

Note: Tear out this page and cut out the clue cards.

Note: Put all the ESL Games from the entire book together for a vocabulary review.

JOB VOCABULARY 1

1. INTERVIEW

2. PERSONNEL MANAGER

3. QUALIFICA- TIONS

4. BENEFITS

5. RÉSUMÉ

6. APPLICATION

JOB VOCABULARY 2

1. RÉSUMÉ

2. OVERTIME

3. FULL–TIME

4. LETTERS OF RECOMMEN–DATION

5. PART–TIME

6. INTERVIEW

6

Debating the Issue

Men and Women in Jobs—A Debate
A Debate—Review

MEN AND WOMEN IN JOBS—A DEBATE

Props: None.

Moderator: Our discussion topic today is "Men and Women in Jobs." I will ask both teams a question before we begin the rebuttal.[1] Each team has one minute to answer. We will begin with Team A. (*To Team A*) In the United States, women earn fifty-nine cents for every dollar a man earns.[2] Should men and women be given equal pay for equal jobs?

Team A: I'd like to answer that by saying that a man must support a family. He must pay the bills. Therefore, men should earn more.

Team A: In addition to what he's said, I'd like to add that a man is physically stronger than a woman. If something heavy needs to be lifted, a man can do it easier.

Moderator: All right. Your time is up. Team B?

Team B: In response to Team A's statement that a man must support a family, I'd like to point out that four out of every ten marriages in the United States end in divorce. In some states, it's even higher. It's necessary for many women to support their own families.

Team B: In general, I think that physical strength is not important on the job. There is nothing to lift in an office except paper or books.

Moderator: Team A can now respond to Team B's arguments.

Team A: In response to the divorce argument, I'd like to look at the situation from the employer's point of view. Let's say a divorced woman has a job with a lot of responsibility. If her children get sick, she has to leave the job to take care of them. What happens if there is an important job to do at work? Who does her work while she's absent?

Team A: Regarding that point, an employer makes an investment when each employee is hired. What if he hires a woman and she gets married and quits? Or becomes pregnant and quits? What happens to his investment?

Moderator: Team B has one minute for final comments.

Team B: Team A has brought up some interesting points, but I think the question was equal pay for equal jobs. If two people are equally qualified and are doing the same job,

---

[1] Rebuttal: response to an opponent's argument (an attempt to prove an opponent's argument incorrect).

[2] Fifty-nine cents for every dollar: 1978, Population Reference Bureau. (Note: This statistic represents an average of all jobs. It does not mean that a woman doing the same job as a man would get fifty-nine cents for every dollar the man gets. In some professions, men and women are paid equally for the same job; in many they are not.)

why shouldn't they receive the same pay? Salaries are not based on need. They are based on job duties and the job's value to society.

Team B: Every employer gambles when he hires an employee. If the employee can't do the job, for whatever reason, the employer has to find someone else. If the employee can do the job, he or she should be paid for the job, not according to sex.

COMPREHENSION

Answer the following questions with your class.

1. What is the question Team A and Team B are debating?
2. Why does Team A think men should earn more money?
3. Why does Team B think there should be equal pay for equal jobs?
4. Which team do you think won the debate and why?
5. Restate the skit in your own words. Use the illustration to help you. **(Tell what happened. Example: The Moderator stated the rules. Then he asked Team A a question, etc.)**

USING VOCABULARY TO COMMUNICATE

ANSWERING QUESTIONS IN A FORMAL DISCUSSION

"These Give You Time to Think"	*"Responding to a Question"*
In general . . . Well, let's see . . . In my opinion . . . From my point of view . . . Actually . . . Well, I think . . .	In response to your question . . . I'd like to answer that by saying . . . With regard to your question, I'd like to say that . . . With regard to that point, I'd like to say that . . . Regarding that point . . .
"Giving Examples"	*"Disagreeing"*
For example . . . Let's say that . . . I'd like to point out that . . . For instance . . .	That's an interesting point, but . . . That's very interesting, but . . . You've brought up some interesting points, but . . . Yes. Well, I think . . .
"Adding More Information"	*"Concluding"*
In addition to what I've already said, I'd like to add . . .	In conclusion, I'd like to say that . . . My perception of the situation is . . . In summary, I'd like to say . . .

Repeat the above after your teacher.

●● **WORK WITH A PARTNER** Use the chart to respond to the following questions or statements. Follow the instructions.

Use "Time to Think" expressions to respond to the question:

1. **You:** Do you think a woman should stay home and a man should work?
   Partner: In my opinion, _____ .

Use "Responding to a Question" expressions to respond to each question:

2. **You:** Four out of ten American marriages end in divorce. How do you feel about that?
   Partner: _____

3. **You:** On the average, American women earn fifty-nine cents for every dollar a man earns. How do you feel about that?
   Partner: _____

Use "Giving Examples" expressions to finish one of the following statements:

4. In my country, men and women do not earn equal pay for equal jobs. (Example) _____ .
   In my country, men and women do earn equal pay for equal jobs. (Example) _____.

Use "Disagreeing" expressions to respond to the statement:

5. **You:** I think men are stronger than women. Therefore, men should be paid more.
   Partner: _____

Use "Concluding" or "Adding Information" expressions:

6. **You:** (Concluding arguments on why men and women shouldn't earn equal pay for the same job) _____
   _____

   Partner: (Concluding arguments on why men and women should earn equal pay for the same job) _____
   _____

●●● **WORK WITH A PARTNER.** Have a discussion. Have your partner finish the sentences, using his own ideas. Then agree, disagree, or comment on what your partner says, using the above chart.

1. **Partner:** I think equal pay for equal jobs _____ .
   You: _____
   Partner: _____
   You: _____
   Partner: _____
   You: _____

2. **Partner:** I think women should _____ .
   You: _____
   Partner: _____
   You: _____
   Partner: _____
   You: _____

3. **Partner:** I think men should _____ .
   You: _____
   Partner: _____
   You: _____
   Partner: _____
   You: _____

4. **Partner:** The problem with the government is _____ .
   You: _____
   Partner: _____
   You: _____
   Partner: _____
   You: _____

5. **Partner:** The best country in the world is _____ because _____ .
   You: _____
   Partner: _____
   You: _____
   Partner: _____
   You: _____

COMMUNICATING YOUR FEELINGS—AN EXPANSION EXERCISE

SUGGESTIONS

	Average	*Strong*
INFORMAL	Speaker 1: Do you want to go? Speaker 2: Yeah. Sure.	Speaker 1: Let's go. Speaker 2: Okay.
FORMAL	Speaker 1: Would you like to leave? Speaker 2: Yes I would.	Speaker 1: Why don't we leave? Speaker 2: That's fine with me. Speaker 1: Would you mind if we left? Speaker 2: Not at all.

Repeat the above after your teacher.

WORK WITH A PARTNER. Make appropriate suggestions to your partner, and have him give appropriate responses. Use the chart on page 118 to help you.

1. You and your partner are having dinner in a very expensive restaurant. You notice that you're the only two customers still there.
   You: Why don't we leave?
   Partner: That's fine with me.

2. You and your partner are having lunch in the school cafeteria. You're both finished with your lunches.
   You: _____
   Partner: _____

3. You and your partner are at a loud party. Someone says the police are coming.
   You: _____
   Partner: _____

4. You want to visit your aunt after school. You want your partner to come too.
   You: _____
   Partner: _____

5. You want your partner to have dinner tonight with your family.
   You: _____
   Partner: _____

ONE STEP FURTHER

Discuss the following questions in small groups. Choose a discussion leader to report back to the class when you finish.

1. Does a man's job make him masculine or can he be masculine no matter what he does? What is masculinity?

2. Does a woman's job (or lack of job) make her feminine? What is femininity?

3. Can a husband and wife both have jobs? If they can, whose job is more important, the husband's or the wife's? Why?

4. Group activity: What is success? Is success the same for a man and a woman? Describe a successful man and then describe a successful woman. Use full sentences. (Example: A successful man has a good education, etc.)

Read your descriptions to the class. Which group's description is best? Why?

5. Group activity: Society values some jobs more than others. For this reason, the salary for some jobs is higher than for others. Look at the following list of jobs. Decide on a salary for each job. Give a reason for each decision. (Why so much? Why so little?)

Job	Starting Salary (per month)	Reason
Truck driver	_____	_____
Doctor	_____	_____
Secretary	_____	_____
President of the United States	_____	_____
Famous rock musician	_____	_____
Teacher	_____	_____
Dentist	_____	_____
Policeman	_____	_____
Garbage collector	_____	_____
U.S. Senator	_____	_____
Lawyer	_____	_____
Famous actress/actor	_____	_____
Engineer	_____	_____
Plumber	_____	_____
Electrician	_____	_____
Psychologist	_____	_____
Salesperson	_____	_____
Business executive	_____	_____
State Congressman	_____	_____

If possible, find out how much people with these jobs really earn. How do the real salaries compare to your group's salaries?

A DEBATE—REVIEW

A DEBATE—REVIEW

Work in a group. Decide on a topic you'd like to debate. Using the previous skit as an example, write your own debate. How many vocabulary words from the previous skits can you use here?

Props: fill in as necessary.

Moderator: _____

Team A: _____

_____ : _____

_____ : _____

_____ : _____

_____ : _____

_____ : _____

_____ : _____

_____ : _____

_____ : _____

_____ : _____

_____ : _____

_____ : _____

_____ : _____

_____ : _____

COMPREHENSION

Answer the following question:

Describe each group's debate. In each case, which team do you think "won" the debate?

ONE STEP FURTHER

Each group should make up its own questions for the other groups to answer.

1. _____

2. _____

3. _____

4. _____

5. _____